STRANGE STORIES
OF CORNWALL

BOSSINEY BOOKS

ACKNOWLEDGEMENTS
Front cover photography: Ray Bishop
Back cover photography: Ray Bishop
Other photographs: Ray Bishop; Felicity Young
Drawings: Felicity Young
Front cover design: Maggie Ginger

ISBN 0 948158 75 1

First published in 1992 by Bossiney Books, St Teath, Bodmin, Cornwall.

Typeset and printed by Penwell Print Ltd, Callington, Cornwall.

STRANGE STORIES OF CORNWALL

S TRANGE stories seemingly grow out of the landscape of Cornwall.

What was it C.C. Vyvyan said of the Cornish atmosphere? 'It never beckons you on and on with unfulfilled promise. All the time it is close to you ... a peculiar intimacy between man and nature ...'

Here, six writers, living and working in Cornwall, two making their debut for Bossiney, prove that fact is often stronger than fiction. The poet Frances Bellerby warned us: 'The bones of this land are not speechless' and she was right, for here in Cornwall the past is at our elbow continuously day and night.

Beauty comes with dawn and that beauty changes as the sun climbs and the shadows move. At noon the colours on the land and in the sea are more clearly defined – on good days at least – yet even then description and definition are complex. The moods are numerous and various.

Cornwall is a natural breeding ground for eccentricity for we, men and women, natives as well as outsiders, who have had deep and sometimes tortuous love affairs with Cornwall.

Parsons of individuality have been legion. Densham at Warleggan on the fringe of Bodmin Moor shaped cardboard figures to people his empty pews. In his Service Book he wrote 'No fog, no wind, no rain – no congregation.' Another, the Perpetual Curate of Gunwalloe, genuflecting when passing the stalls gangway of a London theatre, was told 'You're not at the Mass,' – to which he sharply retorted: 'Everything's Mass to me!'

Down in the Hundred of Penwith was another eccentric clergyman: the Rev. William Spry who served Sennen and St Levan but lived at Penzance nearly ten miles away. He was curate from 1816 to 1826 and travelled on a wooden horse, propelled by his feet along the ground! His dog, Sport, who went everywhere with him, ran alongside. But if the weather was rough, they stayed at home in Penzance. Such was his neglect that it's said weeds grew in the pews and his surplice turned to rags and iron-mould.

But we must not assume all our Cornish eccentrics are or were distinguished. In my lifetime I have had the luck to know several and all had an influence. My old tutor Edmund Sedding, the most absent-minded character I ever met; Jerry Sweet, a wonderful Port Isaac fisherman who supplied us with fish at Bossiney for years and firmly declined to go 'decimal' believing 'it'll never catch on!' Even after decimalization, Jerry still gave us our bill in pounds, shillings and pence. There was that great Tintagel philosopher Allen Menhennick, Allen was a County Council workman, but I still rate him a philosopher. Typical of the man was when a holiday visitor complained about the wet weather. 'Look, mister,' said Allen quietly, 'there are lots of people up in Tintagel churchyard who would love to feel the rain on their faces.' Yes, Allen was a philosopher and an incredible fund-raiser for charities. Throughout his life he must have sold hundreds of thousands of raffle tickets for hundreds of charities. Allen deserved a place in *The Guinness Book of Records* and lesser people have found themselves in the New Year's Honours List.

Then there was Syd Rice, dairyman, another North Cornwall philosopher. Syd, unlike William Spry, was never deterred by bad weather. He gave a personal service second to none; delivering his milk and cream irrespective of the condition of the roads. Snow or ice never stopped Syd. He also had the knack of getting the heart of any complex matter in a few commonsense sentences. Tintagel Chapel was packed for his funeral; and we all felt we had lost a good friend and ally.

June Lander, in her *Eccentrics in Cornwall*, published by Bossiney in 1983 and long out of print, touched on Cornwall's habit of going against the tide:

'There have always been rebels in Cornwall not willing to conform. In 901, Edwin the Elder founded the bishopric of Crediton,

annexing it to Pawton, Callington and Lawhitton 'that the bishop might thrice a year visit the Cornish to extirpate their errors' – for many still apparently resisted Catholic authority, and clung to the customs of the old British church. This 'clinging to the church' was a recurring feature up to the time of Methodism, which obviously appealed to the Cornish, because they flocked to it in droves.

'The unlikely combination of a lawyer and a blacksmith brought about the Cornish rebellion of 1497 when the Cornish Army marched on London. Three months later, the Cornish swam against the tide when they supported Perkin Warbeck after he landed near Land's End and proclaimed himself Richard IV, and again when they were largely for the King's cause in the Civil War.'

In Cornwall you cannot escape John Wesley and you cannot begin to understand Cornwall without reference to him.

Without Methodism, vital pieces are missing from the jigsaw puzzle of Cornish personality. Ours may be a pagan landscape – in places you may rightly feel that the Devil himself presides and *know* that the black arts were practised – but basically we are Celts: emotional and instinctive. Religion of a kind is bred into the bone. Here in Cornwall Wesley won converts by the hundred. "Many of the lions are become lambs ..." he wrote in his *Journal*.

After Wesley came a whole army of Nonconformist preachers. Appropriately Diana Mudd, in her Bossiney debut, recalls two such men.

My favourite Nonconformist story concerns the Old Methodist Meeting House in the village of Altarnun. According to Lionel Pooley, a prominent local Methodist and a letter dated March 2 1864, midway through a meeting one evening, the beam slipped out of the wall, sending the floor and all assembled crashing into the stabling below. An eye-witness recalled that some were calling out: 'Where is my dear sister?' and some were calling out 'Where is my dear brother?' and others: 'Where is my dear husband?' but nobody was asking 'Where is my dear wife?' At the time of the accident a pub, called the Ring of Bells, stood next door. Hearing the noise, the landlord dashed from his bar, and standing at the entrance of the stabling called out: 'I see the Devil have got 'ee!'

Our other new Bossiney author, John Hocking, as befits a former policeman, delves into crime, asking 'Who killed Loveday Lean?'

6

Though Cornwall has had no murderer to compare with the great characters of crime like Jack the Ripper, ancient and modern, Burke and Hare – or Crippen – we have had more than our share of killing.

The only murderer I ever met was a Cornishman and a cricketer. I was scoring for Cornwall and at lunch sat next to a young man called Miles Giffard. We said little to one another. He was due to bat immediately after the interval, and I guessed he was preoccupied. Little did I realize that one day he would batter his parents to death with an iron pipe and wheelbarrow them over a cliff. After their murder Miles drove straight to London and proposed to his girlfriend Gabrielle – who provisionally accepted. His trial took place at Bodmin Assizes in 1953. His defence aimed to prove him insane but forty years ago judges and juries took rather less notice of schizophrenia. He was found guilty and hanged.

Come, let us begin our *Strange Stories of Cornwall*. We shall meet again presently.

Michael Williams
St Teath
February 1992

About the author . . .

DAVID MUDD says he has had to wait 22 years to write his story about Anne Jefferies – 'even in these enlightened times, an M.P. can't write about fairies without attracting a few cutting comments', he says.

Writer, journalist and author before and during his period of service as M.P. for Falmouth & Camborne from 1970-1992, David hopes that he will now be free to write about some of the people and topics that have been taboo for more than two decades. Described in one reference book as a 'craggy Cornish charismatic character' he enjoys writing about the people and incidents embodied in each of the four words written about himself.

Over the years, David Mudd has made a considerable contribution to the Bossiney list – as many as a dozen titles. Around and About The Smugglers' Ways, *published in 1991, was Bossiney's 200th title. Working through almost forty different sources, including the records of H.M. Customs & Excise itself, David discovered in the course of his research that his great-grandfather was a Customs officer. Also in print are* The Cruel Cornish Sea *and* Around and About The Fal.

DAVID MUDD

THE GIRL WHO WAS FED BY THE FAIRIES

David Mudd

THE TIME:	-	The 1600s
THE PLACE:	-	St. Teath
THE CHARACTERS:	-	Moses Pitt, a printer.
		Jan Tregeagle, a magistrate.
		Mary Martin, aged four.
		Anne Jefferies, a servant girl.
		Six persons of small stature, all clothed in green.

THE 17th century was as much a time of upheaval, suspicion, superstition and insecurity in Cornwall as it was in England itself. There would be a civil war; King Charles would be beheaded; Oliver Cromwell would come and go; the Roman Catholic faith would give way to Protestantism; nonconformists would be persecuted; Charles II would reintroduce gaiety after the austerity of Cromwell; James II would be succeeded by William of Orange; there would be the Great Plague and the Fire of London; the Dutch fleet would sail arrogantly up the Thames and down again; Baptists and Quakers would live in fear; and, in a spectacular U-turn, Thomas Lamplugh, Bishop of Exeter, would forget his instruction to Cornish clergy to 'remain loyal to James II and spurn William of Orange' (while James was still on the throne) and urge them to pledge for William of Orange within days of William landing at Brixham.

And, of course, Bishop Trelawny had been in keep and hold at the behest of King James' men.

At St. Teath the 'new' church had been consecrated and was in use, some of the stones of the former Norman church already recycled in the lofty arch of the gabled building in the churchyard. Noted as 'St. Teth, a parishe in the "Alphabeticall Table of Trig Hundred" ' in John Norden's 1584 'Generall Perambulation and Delineation of Cornwall', the village was destined to change its position by up to five miles on the maps of the next century because it was off the main road and not on any of the main routes of communication.

But Anne Jefferies, Moses Pitt, Mary Martyn and Jan Tregeagle were to make it a very famous place indeed.

Moses Pitt, a native of St. Teath, went to London as a haberdasher. He turned his hand to become a publisher with, it seems, a hankering to correspond with the important and influential personages of his day, more especially the then Bishop of Gloucester.

Jan Tregeagle, by repute, by legend and by performance was one of Cornwall's most inglorious sons. He was steward to the Robartes family and a man of outstanding evil, cruelty, wickedness, self-indulgence and duplicity. He exploited every opportunity for self-advancement and self-enrichment on the simple argument that if society consists of exploiters and the exploited, it is better to be an active and fully paid-up member of the former rather than of the latter. He was appointed to the magistracy because he undoubtedly warmed to the authoritarianism of the Cromwellian cause and because, other than in his own reputed flirtations and deals with the devil, he had a disbelief and fear – almost a paranoia – of anything that did not have a rational explanation or, alternatively, posed a threat to what he perceived as a normal and organised way of life.

Mary Martyn, aged four, was the daughter of Humphry Martyn who, it seems, was related to the Pitt family. She was to receive a unique gift.

Anne Jefferies, the daughter of a poor labourer, was born at St. Teath in 1626. While she was working in the Pitt household a remarkable series of events (involving the 'six persons of small stature, all clothed in green') took place.

In 1645, when she was 19, the clouds of civil war were gathering on the horizon. The fact that much of Cornwall would side with the King, and the rest with Oliver Cromwell would have caused her little concern. She was regarded as a remarkably bright and warm girl when in the custom of those days, she entered the household of the

11

Pitts as a servant.

Traditionally the wealthy households would provide a job for the children of the poor. In return for duties performed, the household would provide food and clothing as well as a basic education.

However, Anne had a couple of surprises in store for the Pitts. Firstly, although she was warm, friendly and delicate, she was a tom-boy. Secondly, although she was a tom-boy, her great obsession was to wander through the gardens of the Pitt home in search of fairies with whom, she said, she would like to communicate!

There was, admittedly, nothing outrageous in this in that everyone believed in the little people. Good luck could be attributed to them . . . and they could conveniently equally be blamed for everything that went wrong. But Anne did go further than most people. Not only did she want to meet one, but she wanted to find out just who and what they were and what they did to justify their existence.

It was this extended curiosity that was to lead her into trouble, as Moses Pitt told the Bishop of Gloucester in a letter some 50 years later and by which time, sadly, Anne's own memory had become more than a little clouded both by what she had endured as well as by the fear that she might be ridiculed or exploited.

Moses told the Bishop, in a letter dated May 1 1699 that – one day in 1645 – while walking in the garden, Anne had come across 'six persons of small stature all clothed in green, which she called "fairies", upon which she was so frightened that she fell into a convulsive fit'.

She was taken indoors and, as she came out of the fit, told the amazed family that the small visitors had just gone out of the window! 'And thus in the height of her sickness she would often cry out, and that with eagerness, which expressions were attributed to her distemper, supposing her light-headed'.

There is little doubt that Anne had been seriously ill. The Bishop was told: 'She being at that time so very sick that she could not stand on her feet; and also the extremity of her sickness, and the long continuance of her distemper, had almost perfectly moped (weakened) her so that she became almost as a changeling; and as soon as she began to recover, or to get a little strength, she in her going would stretch her legs as wide as she could and so lay hold with her hands on tables, forms, stools etc., till she had learned to go about again; and if anything vexed her, she would fall into her fits and continue in them for a long time, so that we were afraid she would have died in one of them'.

Two things were significant in this account. Firstly, the suggestion that her behaviour had become unseemly and unladylike. Secondly, the use of the word 'changeling'.

If a child had an unpleasant nature, it was always believed that, at birth, evil fairies or demons had taken the true well-mannered child away and switched it for an ill-tempered one.

Certainly, as she recovered, Anne Jefferies gave obvious signs that her original character had changed.

She was always up to mischief. She could not be left alone for fear that she would cause damage or even set fire to the house. It was widely believed that she had encountered demons rather than fairies and that the agonies of her fits and fevers had been a battle for her soul between good and evil.

Perhaps surprisingly to many people, she went to St. Teath church to give thanks for her recovery. As she regained her health, her strength and her fitness, she began to preach although virtually unable to read.

To many people it was a miracle. To others it was a classic case of a soul being possessed by the devil.

One afternoon, Mrs Pitt had to take a hamper of food to where labourers were harvesting. To be on the safe side, she persuaded Anne to sit out in the garden while she was away. She was thus able to secure the house against possible damage or arson if Anne took one of her 'turns'.

On the way back, Mrs Pitt tripped and injured her leg. She lay at the roadside for several hours until she was discovered and carried home.

To her amazement, Anne was ready and waiting. It was as if she had been given a premonition of the accident.

Telling her mistress not to worry about calling the surgeon, Anne Jefferies took the injured leg in her lap and, by stroking it, soothed the pain and reduced the swelling.

Asked why she had been ready for Mrs Pitt's return, she said that half-a-dozen 'friends' had told her what had happened and how to prepare.

From that day forward, Anne Jefferies became widely sought-after and consulted as a faith-healer by people from London to Land's End. With her fairy friends aiding her she performed many authenticated 'miracle' cures of 'people with all distempers, sores and agues', the Bishop was told many years later. She accepted no money for her work and neither bought, made nor used any medicines, ointments or potions. She 'merely wanted them not as she had occasion'.

As a proof that the fairies could indeed answer all her needs, she refused all offers of food from the Pitt family and their friends for a period of three months. She was, she said, adequately catered-for by her small friends. Moses Pitt wrote of the end of the fast when, on Christmas Day 'she came to our table and said because it was that day she would eat some roast beef with us'. Wondering as to what food was provided by the fairies, Moses went to her room and tasted a piece of bread she claimed the fairies had brought. It was, he said, 'I think the most delicious bread that ever I did eat both before and since'.

Trying to catch her out, a guest went to her locked room. After peeping through the keyhole he returned triumphantly to say that he had been unable to see her and that she must have a secret way out.

Unaware of this, Anne Jefferies joined the family a little while later and said that while she had been with the fairies, one of them had seen the guest looking in through the keyhole.

There was no secret way in or out.

In 1693, Humphry Martyn, a distant relation of the Pitt family, visited Anne Jefferies on the strength of the letter to the Bishop. She greeted him courteously but regretted that she could not tell him of the influence and interventions of the fairies in her life; of her experiences; or of the cures she had performed. She told him: 'If I should discover it to you, I would not have my name spread about the country were I to have £500, and you would make books or ballads of it'. She told Humphry Martyn that she had been questioned 'before justices, and at the sessions, and in prison, and also before the judges at the assizes'.

Perhaps fearing that the interviewer might disbelieve her, Anne

14

DEMONS OR FAIRIES … Which did Anne Jefferies encounter during the battle for her soul?

THE SQUARE · ST TEATH

A FAMOUS PLACE … St Teath. Postcard kindly loaned by Mrs Davey of St Teath.

Jefferies gave him a surprise souvenir for his four-year-old daughter. It was a tiny silver cup from the fairies, inscribed with the name 'Mary Martyn'. It was, she said, a gift from her little friends.

Her dread of attracting the attention of official inquisitors was soundly based as, 48 years earlier in 1645, she had been arrested by constables acting for Jan Tregeagle. Even then she was not taken unawares. When the officers arrived, they found her ready, dressed and prepared to accompany them to Bodmin. She had, she said, been told to expect them.

To test the claims that Anne Jefferies could exist only on food provided by fairies, Tregeagle ordered that she be kept in solitary confinement and under the sole supervision of a warder who could not be bribed, threatened or cajoled into allowing food to reach her.

Moses Pitt told the Bishop: 'and she was so kept. And yet she lived and that without complaining'.

Suspecting that there might be a secret source of food reaching her, Tregeagle had her moved to his own home that he could better guarantee her fast. Once more she showed no signs of starvation.

She was interrogated endlessly in the hope that she might admit to heresy or witchcraft. Once more her small friends helped her when, on the last morning of her judicial examination, they opened her Bible on the page on which is written 'Dearly beloved, believe not every spirit, but try the spirits whether they be of God'.

As an additional aid, they turned down the top corner of the right page so that she could find the text immediately.

She was then discharged from prison on condition that she did not return to the Pitt household.

Although the main implication of Moses Pitt's letter to the Bishop was that Anne's incarceration and interrogation were linked to her association with the little people, papers discovered in the Bodleian Library, Oxford, by the great Cornish social historian A.K. Hamilton Jenkin would seem to suggest that this was not so and that, following her release, Anne was considered to be a potentially subversive influence at a time of growing political and religious upheaval.

The papers hinted that her detention and questioning were more motivated 'lest her discourses (which were all on behalf of the King and strangely saucy against Parliament) should trouble the People's minds who are apt to revolt from the Parliament's obedience'.

Indeed, she was treated with great caution. 'She hath been before the Committee and she bids them do well in their office for it will not last long. She hath been examined by three able Divines, and gives a good account of her religion and hath the Scriptures very perfectly (though quite unlearned). They are fearful to meddle with her, for she tells them to their faces that none of them are able to hurt her . . . She prays very much and bids the people keep the old form of prayer. She says that the King shall enjoy his own, and be revenged on his enemies'.

There are, therefore, two conflicting views of Anne Jefferies. One is as a mystic and faith healer; the other as being politically motivated.

Yet, despite the immense gulf and contradiction of these classifications, the fact remains that there was something beyond human explanation in her powers of overcoming the rigours of fasting and starvation, as well as in her powers of healing.

But if she was no more than a borderline heretic, then why should Moses Pitt have chosen to write to the Bishop some 50 years after the main events had happened?

Sadly, his motives can be questioned. He was up to his eyeballs in debt; his business was on the rocks; he was being pressed by the creditors of a man for whom he had stood surety; he had served time in the notorious Fleet debtors' prison.

Perhaps the crowning of William of Orange persuaded him that the story of Anne Jefferies was a valuable commodity if he could capitalise on it. And how better to set the ball rolling than through an open letter to a leading Bishop?

However, even the authorities who questioned her accepted that she had seen 'six persons of small stature, all clothed in green'.

But were those tiny creatures of the flesh, or of the mind? Had she seen them before her fit, or after her fit, or during her fit? Were they part of a great reality, or were they hallucinations of fever and convulsive fit?

Only the fairies can tell.

About the author . . .

JOHN HOCKING *served in the Cornwall Constabulary for 25 years and wrote a book* In The Name of The Law *about his experiences as a country policeman.*

He has written accounts of various Cornish murders for national crime magazines, and had numerous articles published on a wide variety of subjects – particularly travel.

His short stories were a regular feature in the Police Review. *His latest book: 'A Dozen Cornish Murders' is complete and he is seeking a publisher.*

A long standing member of the Lanner Writers' Group, John is now retired and living at Camborne.

Here he makes his debut for Bossiney, recalling a strange Cornish murder.

JOHN HOCKING

WHO KILLED LOVEDAY LEAN?

John Hocking

IN THE year 1839 the land of Cornwall was honeycombed with hundreds of working tin mines. The stark granite engine houses with their tall round stacks were as much a part of Cornwall as its sturdy independent people.

Miners with huge pasties made of barley, and a bottle of cold tea in their 'crowse bags' blew out the tallow candles lighting their cottages at four or five am and began their long trudge along the cliff tops and muddy lanes for distances of up to seven and eight miles to mines with names like Wheal Jewell, Ding Dong, Tresavean, and Wheal Charlotte.

There were no cages to ride swiftly down the shafts to the 'level'. They descended by greasy wooden ladder into the depths and after ten hours labour with pick and shovel they climbed wearily back up for the long walk home. In the remaining hour or so of daylight they smoked a pipe over the garden gate and tended their vegetable patch, after which, too weary to stay up longer they fell into bed with only another early start and backbreaking day to look forward to.

Such was the unenviable drudgery of the Cornish miner in the year 1839.

Jesse Lean was a miner and carrier who lived in the hamlet of Trevarth in the parish of Gwennap. He and his wife Loveday, both elderly, had worked hard to keep body and soul together. As a result they were slightly better off than some because Jesse owned and hired out a couple of horses as well.

Jesse was an early riser and at five o'clock on the bitterly cold morning of February 8 1839 he got up, leaving his wife in bed and went out to the stable.

21

WEARISOME WORK … They descended by greasy wooden ladder into the depths.

The horses snorted in recognition and clumped their hooves against the cobble floor. After busying himself for a little while cleaning up and feeding the horses, he went back inside to the rear kitchen. Jesse made himself a cup of tea and buttered a thick slice of his wife's home-made loaf. As he sat at the table enjoying his quiet early breakfast he heard somebody lift the latch of the front door.

'Who's there?' he called.

There was no answer, and when he opened the door, he saw no one although he did hear a footstep. He looked out of the front door into the bright moonlight and heard the clatter of hobnailed boots. A fellow miner, Stephen Jeffery was coming down the road.

'Have'ee seen anybody?' enquired Jesse.

'Well, yes I have,' said Jeffery. 'I seen a man running pretty fast with his head down, but I couldn't see his face close enough to recognise. He had on a blue or dark coat and seemed to me a brave hardy youngster'.

Jesse went back inside, pondering this information as he tried to light a fire, but couldn't get it going properly. Loveday, his wife came down the stairs and got busy with it. 'A typical man, Jesse,' she told him fondly, 'can't get a bit of stick going!'

Soon, the fire flickering cheerfully in the cold stone kitchen, Loveday busied herself seeing that her husband had his pasty and bottle of tea packed in his haversack. She saw him off with a peck on the cheek saying, 'I think I'll go back to bed for a while dear – till the room do warm up a bit.'

'All right for thee,' grumbled Jesse as he picked up his haversack and set off for Wheal Jewell.

Samuel Trengove, a man in his thirties who lived a little further up the road from Jesse, unable to work underground because of an accident, counted himself lucky to have a part-time job as the driver of Jesse's horses. Sammy came to the house at a quarter to seven and was startled to hear Mrs Lean upstairs 'wailing fit to beat the band'.

'Is that you Sammy?' she called, 'I'm dying Sammy – go and fetch your mother do!' Now thoroughly alarmed, Samuel Trengove hurried away to fetch his mother and then set off to Wheal Jewell where he told the shift boss what had occurred and suggested that

THE FLEEING MURDERER … The man glimpsed running from Loveday Lean's cottage.

Jesse Lean should return home without delay.

Meanwhile, Sammy's wife Grace had arrived at the Lean's cottage and went upstairs to the bedroom. Loveday Lean lay half out of the bed, ghastly stab wounds disfigured her face and neck. Everything was covered with blood.

'Oh – I'm dying! How is my face so stiff? Send for the doctor do. How am I like this? How is all the blood here?'

'My dear Loveday – who have done this?' asked the shocked and terrified Mrs Trengove.

'I heard the door creak and a man come in,' said Loveday. 'I couldn't see his face and he scat me over the eye with something – oh my dear Lord!'

The surgeon, Mr Mitchell, arrived, and noted there was a 'great effusion of blood' on the right side of her face and neck. On the right side of her face there were three stab wounds and another in the ear, made by a sharp instrument.

The surgeon applied a lotion and promised to call again later.

Jesse had by now hurried home and rushing upstairs clasped his wife to his arms. He comforted her and held her for most of the night. Loveday remained conscious until half past ten that night, but she died at about nine o'clock on Thursday morning. Her last words to her husband were, 'My dear, come to bed so I can turn to you.'

The Coroner's inquest was held next day, Friday, at the house of Mr Whitburn at Gwennap.

'It belongs to the Magistrates,' said a report at the time, 'not merely to receive such evidence as may be offered them, but to search for the guilty party and for the proofs by which this offence might be brought home to him.'

There were no police to be involved, and it was left to the magistrates, and the vicar of the parish, the Rev Thomas Phillpots to pursue enquiries. At the inquest more strange and contradictory facts were put forward to add to the mystery.

Cross examined, Jesse Lean said that there was no property missing from the house, but that he suspected a local man, William White, a ne'er do well and part- time miner, of stealing eggs. Jesse had once ordered him off the premises. He was therefore a possible suspect.

PEACEFUL PLOT … Loveday was buried in Gwennap churchyard.

White, of Trevarth cottage, was brought before the inquest, where he was questioned probingly by the magistrates. He told the inquest that he had just gone to live with his father-in-law, Mathew Mills, and had moved in with him on the day of the murder at about seven o'clock in the morning.

'Why did you move in with your father-in-law?'

'Well – I was out of work and had been living with my grandfather and had no money for my keep so I moved in with father-in-law. Now though, since Thursday I've got a job over at Wheal Jewell.'

'I would like you to account for your movements. What were you doing on the Tuesday – the day prior to the murder?' the Chairman asked.

'I left my grandfather's house after breakfast and went over to Consul mine looking for work.'

'And after that?'

'Afterward I went to Lanner and slept in Will Martin's barn. I didn't have the nerve to go back to my grandfather's house, even though I had been without meat since the day before.'

'So you spent the Tuesday night in the barn – and then?'

'I left the barn at about five o'clock and walked to John Paul's blacksmith's shop. I was afraid to go back to grandfather's house.'

'What were you afraid of?'

'Lest he should thrash me for staying out all night. That's how after, I went to my father-in-law's house and stayed there all day on Wednesday.'

White said he had not been on Jesse Lean's premises for three or four years and asserted Lean had never ordered him off.

John Paul, the blacksmith, said that he knew White and said that he had been at his shop on Thursday morning but not Wednesday as White had stated.

William Nicholls, a miner of Gwennap, said that he had passed the Lean's cottage early on Wednesday morning, when he had heard someone groaning and crying to the Lord for mercy.

'What did you do as a result of hearing this?' asked the Coroner.

'Well sir – I just stood there – took aback you might say for a few minutes, and then Mrs Betsy Martin came along. I said to her, "Betsy – you're a Methodist. Go and see what you can do for the

MINING RELIC … Jesse Lean worked at Wheal Jewell mine.

Lord's sake." Betsy Martin wouldn't go in there and said it was none of her business. Then suddenly we heard a noise like somebody jumping out of bed. I said to Betsy "Come on – I suppose she have found the Lord now" and we went off together.'

Nicholls further stated that on the previous Sunday he had gone with William White into Jesse Lean's stable, where Lean was cleaning the horses. They had a bit of a chat, he said.

Betsy Martin testified: 'It sounded as if there was only one person and that she was praying. I know I should have gone in there, but I was frightened.'

Uriah Penaluna of Wendron, a 'stamp man' at Tresavean Mine said that White came into the stamp house on Tuesday night to warm himself up. He stayed until four o'clock when Penaluna told him he had better go.

The next witness was Harold Prior, a miner of Gwennap. He met White near Lean's house at seven o'clock on Wednesday morning, going along the great road from Trevarth. He had his head well down, as if hiding his face as he walked along.

Jesse Lean told the inquest that on the previous Tuesday evening, at tea time, he heard a sound in the back kitchen and called out 'Who's there?' Some one with a youthful voice answered – 'Can you lend me a horse tomorrow?'

'I don't know you – who are you?' Jesse called back. He went back into the kitchen with a light, and found the door wide open. He saw a man running away and shouted: 'Let me see who you are,' but the man didn't stop.

'When we went to bed that night,' Jesse told the Coroner, 'I said to my wife Loveday, "Look – we have got a bit of money, and we are two old people. No person shall be better off for coming here." Loveday took out the chest and hid it in another part of the house. She did not say how much money there was.'

June Bray, a widow, had been drinking tea with Loveday on the Tuesday night, and fully corroborated Jesse Lean's evidence of the man coming to the back and saying he wanted a horse.

Her testimony closed the evidence, and the Coroner having summed up, let the jury mull over the facts before they found a verdict of wilful murder by person or persons unknown.

By present day standards of investigations, the inquiries into the circumstances of Loveday Lean's murder left much to be desired.

The prime suspect, White, a young drifter and workshy ne'er do well, told a story so full of contradictions that it would certainly have warranted further inquiries today.

Why, for example did White state that he had not been to Lean's premises for three or four years when he was there the previous Sunday with William Nicholls?

How could White have been in the barn and in the stamp house at the same time?

Who lifted the latch of the kitchen door in the still of the early morning?

Whose was the youthful voice that asked: 'Can you lend me a horse?'

Nothing apparently, was missing from the house, and the possibility of it having been ransacked was not mentioned at the inquest.

Could there, on reflection, have been more than one person 'acting in concert' to rob the old couple?

Nobody at any stage was identified as a likely murderer, and no motive was suggested. Jesse and Loveday Lean were considered to be 'better off' than their fellow villagers and may have been thought to have money.

In any event poor Loveday Lean – an innocent Cornish miner's wife – was brutally murdered in her own bed and one hundred and fifty years later, the mystery remains unsolved.

AS THE TREE BENDS … Cornish country lanes hide many secrets.

About the author . . .

FELICITY YOUNG *is a Cornish-based painter who lives at Tintagel with her husband Ian, daughter Hazel, horse Red and dogs Arthur and Digger. She lived in Somerset for more than 20 years and still makes regular visits to the county. She was educated at Lord Digby's Grammar School, Sherborne, Dorset.*

Since 1984 she has contributed more than 250 illustrations for a whole range of Bossiney titles. She recently did a radio broadcast on the craft of illustrating books. A member of the British Horse Society, she rides regularly – and teaches yoga.

In 1989 Felicity made her debut as a Bossiney author, contributing a chapter on Lawrence of Arabia in Dorset Mysteries. *Then in 1990 came her first book* Curiosities of Exmoor. *In 1991 she contributed a chapter in* Strange Dorset Stories, *recalling Charlotte Bryant, a small-time prostitute accused of murdering her husband. Now she explores* Some Strange Places.

SOME STRANGE PLACES

Felicity Young

BARRAS NOSE, TINTAGEL

A DOG can often sense the sinister undercurrent of a place long before we humans are even aware that the site has any mysterious connections or that anything strange has happened there in the past. I am sure that dogs, cats and even horses can pick up vibrations on a different level to us and how they react depends on whether these vibrations are good or evil.

My own dog, Arthur, is an extremely boisterous Welsh Springer Spaniel always full of life when I take him out walking on the cliffs near my home in Tintagel – except when we visit one particular piece of coastline; Barras Nose (or Barras Head) promontory which juts out into the sea below Tintagel Castle ruins. Whenever we approach this spot he tucks in his rather stubby tail and looks behind him furtively almost as if he wished to be gone from that place, sniffing the ground cautiously and never straying far from my side.

To me, Barras Nose has always seemed a pleasant enough place, popular with anglers and walkers, much frequented by visitors as well as by local people. In the summer the gorse is in full bloom, casting a strange scent almost like warm coconut into the air. The vivid yellow flowers attract a multitude of butterflies and bees, the bracken and hosts of other wild flowers carpet the cliffside and make one feel almost welcome. Below, at the foot of the cliffs the sea heaves to and fro, its colour ranging from azure to aquamarine, so transparent it is not unusual to spot the dark shadowy form of a basking shark as it weaves its way lazily through the water. Seals and dolphins too have been sighted here playing in the cold waters off-shore. But for all its beauty Barras Nose still casts fear into my dog.

SCENTING MYSTERY … Arthur on Barras Nose.

A SECRET PAST? … Does the strange atmosphere of Barras Nose emanate from the Dark Ages?

Could the answer lie somewhere back in Tintagel's dark history? This area is certainly one of great archaeological importance. Putting aside the romantic vision of King Arthur which has made it popular with tourists the Castle Island was once the site of a monastic settlement founded by St Julitta as long ago as 500 AD. The castle itself was built much later in 1145 by Earl Reginald, the illegitimate son of King Henry I, and had a chequered history before its decline in the 15th century. Tintagel's history can be traced back beyond 500 AD. During the Iron Age, Barras Nose and Willapark both had fortifications of banks and ditches probably put there by the Celtic people who came over from the continent, and links with the Romans have been discovered in the churchyard and on the hill at Condolden nearby, where there is the site of a Roman camp.

In the hot summer of 1983 a fire burned for days on the island. When the dust finally settled it was discovered that the Castle Island was disclosing its long-held secrets, layer by layer shedding each period of history allowing the archaeologists to delve much deeper than before.

What else will surface in the future, who knows? Perhaps it is the result of this 'disturbance' that has brought a spirit to haunt Barras Nose. Barras is certainly a notorious spot for suicides. It is as if there is an uncanny magnetism which draws its victim. Perhaps this is the message that my dog is receiving, making him all too eager to leave?

Walking down the footpath that leads towards the sea, passing the sombre facade of the Castle Hotel and looking out towards the Castle Island where the skeleton of Tintagel Castle clings to the steep cliffs, you can hardly ignore the awesome atmosphere which pervades this particular piece of North Cornwall. It is easy to become oblivious to the many other walkers using the coastal footpath here. Barras Nose is owned by the National Trust, one of their very first acquisitions in 1897, helping to safeguard our precious coastline. Tintagel, the castle and the adjacent coastline are shrouded in romantic legend, and many who visit are drawn by the claim that this is King Arthur country. Others come to explore the ruins, to revel in the sheer antiquity of the place, both, however, are caught up in Tintagel's unique and magical atmosphere. The imagination can run riot here, whether it be visions of knights in shining

armour or a more down-to-earth perception of those poor people so long ago huddled in their stone and thatched huts sheltering from the sou'westerly wind, with few comforts in their draughty world.

Michael Williams in his recent publication *Supernatural Search in Cornwall* recounts the taking of his terrier Tex to the summit of Roughtor high on Bodmin Moor. When they reached a certain point the dog refused to walk, appearing terrified by some unseen danger.

'The dog's tremors were so violent that I thought he was going to die . . . Did he detect something beyond our human vision that morning?' This may have some bearing on my spaniel's behaviour when he approaches Barras Nose (Tex also behaved strangely here, refusing to go out onto the headland) is it possible that he too can feel a 'presence' which is sinister and unfriendly? Can he detect an evil spirit which haunts this spot, unbeknown to us mere human beings?

BOSSINEY COVE

LEAVING Barras Nose and heading towards Boscastle the coastal footpath drops down sharply, with another even steeper track leading from it to Bossiney Cove. In the summer months this little bay is a hive of activity, not quite enough off the beaten track to deter visitors, its comparative seclusion attracts surfers, swimmers and sunbathers. Perhaps though, all this bustle has made it lose some of its magic. In the middle of winter, however, when most people are at home in front of the fire, a walk down the slippery steps is very rewarding. The cove is small, the towering rocks crowd in, making you feel as tiny as the specks of sand on the beach.

I find the atmosphere here quite awesome, it always has a chill to it even in the summer, when the sun is trying to fry you like a lobster, those dark grey cliffs have no warmth in them. Standing, looking out at the vast Atlantic like a sentinel, is what appears to be a gigantic elephant, the self appointed custodian of Bossiney Cove; this natural 'sculpture' is known as Elephant Rock.

Besides the curious rock formation in the cove, Bossiney has another strange phenomenon. In a sloping field above the steps leading to the beach is a well. In itself not very strange, except that as the water issues from the rock the surrounding vegetation is slowly turned to stone – for this reason it is called the Petrifying Well.

The walk up from the cove is strenuous and in places quite slippery, I can't help imagining the poor donkeys years ago who had to haul their burden of sand up this treacherous path. They belonged to an old fisherman and had to make three trips a day, they were obviously chosen for their sure-footedness.

TURNED TO STONE … The Petrifying Well at Bossiney.

◀ *HOLY WATER … The well dedicated to St Piran.*

INTRIGUING … The little chapel in Trethevy.

ST. PIRAN'S WELL AND CHAPEL, TRETHEVY

CORNWALL could well be called 'The Land of Saints'. One who came in about 490AD was St. Piran, the patron saint of miners and of Cornwall; legend has it that he floated over the sea from Ireland on a millstone! His emblem is the Cornish flag, a black background with a white cross, which can be seen flying on March 5, St. Piran's feast day.

It is strange then to find the tiny hamlet of Trethevy near Tintagel boasting a well and chapel dedicated to such an illustrious saint, whose main connections were much further west.

The little chapel is not really a very remarkable building, looking more like a farm outhouse than a place of worship, in fact this is just what it was for much of its history, until being given back to the church by its then owner, Mr Sidney Harris in 1941. Not much is known about its origins, though some features still surviving lead experts to believe it is a mediaeval chapel. In 1457 parson Gregory then vicar of Tintagel, was licensed to hold mass at Saint Piran's but during the reformation it fell into disuse as a 'House of God' and became a shelter for livestock.

There can still be seen a small lancet window in the east wall and old stories tell of a huge slab being used as an altar. Stone seating surrounded the walls, there is also mention of the mysterious unearthing and reburying of a coffin believed to be that of a saint, altogether making this an intriguing little place. There is a sad, rather ironic note to add to the history of St Piran's. Once the chapel had been restored in 1945 a date was arranged for the first mass to be celebrated there. The mass took place on a bitterly cold Sunday morning in February – most strangely the exact same day that Sidney Harris, the donor of the chapel, died in hospital.

Below the chapel, across the rough track which leads to St. Nectan's Kieve, is the well also dedicated to St. Piran. It is not in very good condition, the stones crumbling and covered in lichen, surmounted by a rusty iron cross, but it is still of interest to pilgrims on the trail of curiosities. The ancient little chapel may not be the most beautiful, nor the well the most significant, but the atmosphere here definitely has a magic of its own.

BODMIN GAOL

WHAT stranger place could there be than an old gaol, a building full of atmosphere, the grief and despair cloying the air, a place where men and women were hanged for, in some cases, committing nothing more than petty theft.

The prison in Bodmin was built in 1778 on a piece of land known as Berrycombe, at a time when the gaol in Launceston was in a serious state of disrepair and the accommodation cramped. Bodmin gaol also suffered from overcrowding by 1820 and it was extended to such an extent that Launceston became obsolete and finally closed in 1829. Bodmin then became the only county gaol. Hangings took place publicly until 1862, then screened from view early in the morning, the last-ever hanging at the gaol being that of a William Hampton for murder on July 20 1909. Here, at Bodmin gaol, men were hanged for stealing a mare, a watch, a sheep, for setting fire to a corn stack or forging a £2 note! Their offences may seem sad and trivial to us now, but crime of any sort was then treated as very serious. Along with the thieves were hanged several murderers.

One well known case is that of Charlotte Dymond who was murdered by her jealous lover one Sunday in 1844. Her body was found near Roughtor ford on Bodmin Moor, where a monument has been erected. Matthew Weeks was accused of her murder, sentenced and hanged on August 12 the same year. Some say poor Charlotte's ghost still walks the barren moorland below Roughtor.

Bodmin Gaol was often a holding place for criminals waiting to be transported to penal colonies overseas. This must have been a desperate time for those men and women, torn away from families and loved ones. The practice of deportation was tantamount to slavery. It was not abolished until the mid-nineteenth century.

Punishment at the gaol was harsh, a large treadmill which ground corn for prison use had to be operated by offending prisoners, even when the corn was ground they still had to tread the mill. The use of the treadmill caused a riot in 1827 but it was successfully quelled, in fact law and order was well kept by the 'turnkeys'

PLACE OF DESPAIR ... The notorious Bodmin Gaol.

throughout the gaol's history.

A grim reminder of the deaths which occurred at the prison from the many hangings was the burial of many bodies at the site.

It is thought that when the gaol was rebuilt, all the bodies which had previously been buried under the coalyard were unearthed and re-buried in the grounds of the new gaol. Perhaps this contributes to the chilly atmosphere present in the building, the place seems to have an overwhelming feeling of sadness, a feeling reported by many who have visited the gaol.

For the men and women under sentence of death, the tolling of the prison bell and the raising of the black flag must have struck fear and despair into their hearts, heralding the end of another life. For the population of Bodmin, a hanging meant a day out and for the tradesmen valuable income from ghoulish sightseers. Thousands were treated to a grandstand view of the macabre proceedings.

The civil prison closed in 1916, it had been used by the naval authorities for some years and continued as a naval prison until 1927 when it was finally ordered to close.

The fortunes of the gaol have been mixed since its closure, changing hands many times, becoming a dance hall and a night-club. Somehow, though, a building that has such connections with death and despair does not strike me as a place where laughter and happiness will ever flourish.

The old cell blocks fall into decay and the memories of the people who lived their last days within the walls disappear with them or do they? A rattling of keys has been heard where the cells once stood, perhaps there are unhappy souls haunting this bleak place with such a past.

RUINS … Temple Church before reconstruction in 1883.

TEMPLE CHURCH

A BARE little church in a moorland combe is a strange place to find a connection with those chivalrous crusaders, the Knights Templar. The tiny church of St. Catherine in the village of Temple on Bodmin Moor was built originally by these illustrious Knights in the twelfth century, a time when they were founding religious establishments in England and Europe.

The building on the site is not the original church. In the 1880s it replaced another which had become derelict and which had been placed on the exact foundations of the one built by the Templars.

The Knights Templar were founded in 1119, one of three great orders of religious knights, the others being the Hospitaliers – later to become the Knights of Malta – and the Teutonic Order. Their purpose was to protect pilgrims journeying to and from Jerusalem and they displayed great courage and devotion during the Crusades becoming identified by their white mantle bearing a red cross. At

REBUILT … The tiny church with knightly connections.

first they were a non-military order but later became soldier-knights and their wealth and power grew. This was to be their downfall. They were subjected to much persecution by kings and popes, jealous of their increasing strength until finally the order was suppressed by Pope Clement V in 1312. Most of their English posses-sions were handed over to the Hospitaliers. Temple church, that simple, quiet place, may not be an original Templars' hospice but there is a strongly-forged link with those valiant knights of old. The stained-glass window above the altar displays the red cross, the emblem of the Crusaders.

The village of Temple, strangely enough, was once the Gretna Green of Cornwall. After the Reformation, this tiny moorland church remained outside the authority of the Bishop – until 1744 anyway – and Carew was moved to record that: 'Many a bad mar-riage bargain is there yearly slubbered up.'

Once a desolate spot, Temple, despite improved roads, remains a strange place – unknown to the average tourist.

ALEX TOR

FOR OUR final destination on this trail of strange places, we move to the other side of the Moor. On leaving the village of St. Breward, heading towards a farmstead called the Candras, you are suddenly plunged into a most unusual landscape. The road, unfenced and bounded only by deep ditches, opens out on to Bodmin Moor and everywhere around, lying carelessly strewn, are granite boulders. It is as if some mighty giant in a fit of rage picked up a handful of gravel and threw it onto the ground below.

Quite at random, the rocks cover a large area, then as suddenly as they begin, they cease. This bleak, eerie part of the moor is near the site of King Arthur's Hall, an ancient earthworks, possibly of mediaeval origins which has somehow become associated with the legendary King. All around are stone circles and settlements; sure indication that at one time this area was quite well populated. Walking there in the loneliness of the moors, it would be very easy to let your imagination run away with you, conjuring up visions of stone huts huddled together sheltering from the fierce winds which blow rain, sleet and snow across these wastelands.

Looking down on this landscape are the well known tors of Roughtor and Brown Willy dominating the skyline, but near to the Candras is a smaller lesser-known but imposing tor: Alex Tor. It is from here that the boulders seem to emanate. Perhaps our mystery giant was standing on the rocky summit of Alex Tor when he hurled his stones, scattering them at his feet. Whatever the explanation as to their origin, they still remain a source of inspiration to those with a vivid imagination. The sheep and ponies grazing on the springy grass seem oblivious to these rocks, meandering between them, sometimes using the larger ones to shelter from the keen wind.

Alex Tor is made up of smooth rounded shapes, piled precariously on top of each other, the immense granite rocks do not give the impression of being very stable, but needless to say they have been this way for thousands of years!

The moor has always been a great attraction to horse riders, the wide open space offering freedom hard to find elsewhere. In these days of intense farming, horses are often unwelcome on fields and tracks, and it is a joy to be able to gallop away from the restriction of a metalled road. However, care must be taken as there are many bogs and hidden dangers lurking. The weather too can be a hazard, it is all too easy to lose your bearings when fog descends, enveloping all the landmarks in a thick blanket. Each year the local riding club hold a race on the moor using Alex Tor as the turning point, a case of round the rocks and back. It's definitely not for the faint-hearted, but it is a thrilling event for all who take part.

As an artist I find myself intrigued by the stark landscape of Bodmin Moor. The barren tracts are broken only by the eruption of huge granite boulders which rise above the Cornish countryside to form the tors. Perching high and precarious they can be seen from miles away, enigmatic and mysterious, they are calling me to pick up my brush and paint.

You can understand, when you look at the shapes created here by nature, where the famous sculptor Dame Barbara Hepworth must have got much of her inspiration. Once again Mother Nature has stimulated painters, sculptors and writers to create and recreate. Alex Tor and its scattering of mystery stones is just a small but brilliant speck in the vast amphitheatre of the Moor.

STREWN BOULDERS … The strange landscape below Alex Tor.

About the author . . .

JOY WILSON was born and bred in Liverpool in pre-Beatle era. She was at school at Merchant Taylors' and then spent four years at Trinity College, Dublin, reading French and English Literature. A year in France teaching was followed by a few months in Leicester where she met Colin Wilson, her husband.

She worked as a librarian in London and then a year after 'The Outsider' was published in 1956 they moved to Cornwall – for six months they thought – but they've been here ever since, making their home at Gorran.

In 1985 Joy contributed a chapter to Westcountry Mysteries, *introduced by her husband Colin. In 1986 she made a major contribution to the Bossiney list* Around St. Austell Bay, *the author's words accompanied by a wealth of old photographs and picture postcards. Then came* East Cornwall in the Old Days – *she again skilfully combined text and old pictures.*

Joy's most recent Bossiney title was Cornwall, Land of Legend *published in 1989, telling the story of Tristan and Iseult.*

Now she tells of the Tragi-Comedy of the Last of the Trevanions – and the creation of Caerhays Castle.

JOY WILSON

THE TRAGI-COMEDY
OF THE LAST
OF THE TREVANIONS

Joy Wilson

ON THE south coast of Cornwall in the beautiful Roseland district is the village of St. Michael Caerhays built close to the ancient church. Below the hilltop on which it stands, the little River Luney flows in a long twisting valley down from its source on the edge of the Cornish moors. Close to the village it passes a thickly wooded slope that was once an ancient deerpark. Then, before it joins the sea the stream curves out into a carefully landscaped serpentine lake. Beyond it, looking out over gently sloping meadows, stands Caerhays Castle, battlemented and picturesque as in a child's fairytale. Seen from the hillside opposite its irregular but perfect silhouette of round and square towers and turrets in a tranquil setting of darker woodland gives no hint of the strange dramas involved in its creation.

Long ago Caerhays was royal territory, in pre-Saxon times probably the seat of a native Cornish king. Later, in mediaeval times these lands came into the possession of the Trevanion family who made their ancestral home here. They held these and other Cornish lands from 1390 in unbroken male descent for twelve generations and the history of the Trevanion family has been closely entwined with the history of Cornwall itself.

Four Trevanion brothers fought at Crecy in the entourage of the Black Prince. Later Sir William Trevanion, knighted at Bosworth Field, rode quickly back home with the approval of the king to seize the lands of his renegade neighbour Sir Henry de Bodrugan, who then fled abroad leaving behind a curse that as well as his lands, the Trevanions should also inherit his own fatal extravagance.

STRONGHOLD ... Caerhays Castle, showing the bottom gate where an army of bailiffs assembled.

But for generations the Trevanion family were to thrive on the revenues of their Cornish lands, both seized and inherited by right. One of them jousted before Henry VIII, while Elizabeth Trevanion who married at court, looked after the infant Charles I. In Civil War times gallant Jack Trevanion died at the siege of Bristol fighting for the Royalist cause. Later his father paid heavy fines to the Puritans but still gave shelter in the family manor house at Caerhays to Royalist conspirators from France who were trying to reinstate the king. Then another Trevanion, a sea captain, carried James II on his ship when he fled overseas to France.

By 1730 the Trevanion family was prosperous enough to wish to embellish its old home at Caerhays, built in Tudor times to replace an even earlier house. Tonkin, an historian who lived close by at Polgorran and suffered from damp in his own house, waspishly commented that, *'John Trevanion bestowed a great deal of money on buildings, gardens etc at Caerhays but as there is nothing of regularity observed, it may more properly be called a pleasant romantic seat than a complete habitation, and although it face south, yet it lies too much under the hill and is therefore cold and damp in winter.'*

Dr Borlase, a kindlier visitor, described the old house as, '. . . *charming, low and rambling, grouped round a courtyard entered under a granite archway, on one side of which was a chapel, its windows of old glass . . .'.* There were curtains of silk, coloured glass with heraldic shields and a parlour all panelled in chestnut and with the royal arms of Mary Tudor carved over the mantel.

With all the improvements to the grounds perhaps the Bodrugan curse of extravagance may have come into play at last. Certainly after twelve generations of uninterrupted male inheritance in the Trevanion line, the dreaded 'curse of the Cornish' also struck, when only daughters were born. One daughter, Sophia, married her cousin Admiral John Byron taking with her a substantial dowry. Her grandchild was the famous poet Byron and with her alliance a certain wild and romantic streak seemed to come into play in the fortunes of the family.

The elder daughter Frances Trevanion inherited Caerhays and all the Cornish estates. She had married a Doctor of Divinity called Bettesworth whose father had been lampooned as a 'booby' by Jonathan Swift. It was one of Frances' grandchildren, John Trevanion Purnell Bettesworth, who came to inherit Caerhays in his turn. As we shall see, like his brother George, he had a much more flamboyant character than his duller Bettesworth relatives. In the new romantic spirit of 1801 when he became 21 he added Trevanion to his name, perhaps in an effort to maintain a closer identity with the ancient family's historic past. Since John Trevanion Purnell Bettesworth Trevanion was such a mouthful he became generally known as JTPB.

Inside the little Norman church of St. Michael on the top of a hill just inland from where the present castle stands, there is the Trevanion aisle, originally built by the family in the fifteenth century. There, among the slate and marble family monuments is a life-size black statue with an ebony-like surface, of a handsome young naval officer of Napoleonic times. He stands in heroic pose, a long sword grasped in his right hand, anchor and large cannon at his foot and battle flag draped triumphantly over his shoulder. No inscription gives a clue to his identity and his history is largely forgotten

THE BLACK BOY ... A hero remembered in Caerhays Church.

SMUGGLERS' COASTLINE … The view from the coastguard's watch tower.

today but this young man, Captain George Byron Bettesworth, was in his time a national hero as well as being the admired younger brother of JTPB.

George Bettesworth was the youngest sea captain in Nelson's navy. He was commissioned at 20 as captain of the frigate *Crocodile* after a heroic episode when aged 18, he had taken command of the ship though badly wounded himself, after his captain was killed. Acclaimed by the entire nation he was rewarded by the government with an honorary sword, a unique event, and was one of Nelson's 'Band of Brothers'. When frigate captains were the eyes and ears of the navy keeping watch on the enemy, he carried important despatches from Nelson back to the Admiralty telling of the French navy's movements – the prelude to the battle of Trafalgar. His cousin the poet Byron boasted in a letter to a friend that he expected to, *'go to sea for four or five months with my cousin Capt. Bettesworth who commands the finest frigate in the navy. We are going to the Mediterranean or to the West Indies or to the Devil for if there is a possibility of taking me there Bettesworth will do it . . .'*

But fate struck and ended what might have been a great naval career when George Bettesworth's ship was becalmed, then ambushed and sunk in the cold northern waters off Norway just after the battle of Copenhagen in 1808.

His brother JTPB was left disconsolate and, in time, to comfort the family commissioned the elegant statue in his brother's memory. Interestingly, it was made of a new material, Coade's Patent Stone of strange composition which perhaps we shall encounter again.

For JTPB was himself also precocious in talent. Aged only 24, as the Trevanion heir he had been made Sheriff of Cornwall. Then in 1806 he was elected Whig MP for Penryn when Sir Christopher Hawkins had to retire in disgrace since it was proved that he had bought all the votes in his favour at 24 guineas apiece. As he had also supplied free drinks all round his expenditure was considered excessive. However this Whig parliament proved shortlived and achieved little and JTPB did not stand again.

Instead he turned his abundant energies in a new direction. Perhaps he felt a strong need to try to equal the heroic exploits of his dead sailor brother with achievements of his own that would be in tune with the fashion of the new Romantic age.

While in London he had met John Nash, the architect of Regent Street and later of the Brighton Pavilion and Buckingham Palace. JTPB grandly commissioned him to create for himself a new country seat at Caerhays that would be worthy of the great Trevanion heritage. It was to be a building in the new Gothic style, a re-creation of a mediaeval stronghold. No expense was to be spared – there was a national economic boom at the time due to the war with Napoleon. Nash duly designed for him a picturesque dream of a Gothic castle with battlements, perfect in its setting in a newly landscaped park, with a manmade lake and elegant terraces surrounding the irregular curves and angles of the mock mediaeval walls. Sadly, the old Trevanion family manor house that had stood there so long was to be totally destroyed, its site reused with little thought of all the history encapsulated in its ancient walls, now lost for ever. No doubt the local Cornish people welcomed the extra employment the construction of the new building provided but surely they must have marvelled at the unCornishness of it and the extravagance of all the expenditure.

For it was not long before financial problems arose. Although Nash was one of the most imaginative architects of his time and unequalled in creating beautiful exteriors to the buildings he designed, he also had a slipshod side to his character. It never occurred to him to visit Cornwall and the Caerhays site. Airily he gave orders for the use of experimental materials in important parts of the castle structure, totally failing to take into account the stresses imposed by the rains and windstorms of a typical Cornish winter. Perhaps he used the same material as that used for the 'black boy' memorial statue up in the church, whose composition is still a puzzle today.

When at last the long war with Napoleon ended a slump began in earnest. Cornish rents, fishing tithes and dues from tin mining, all were reduced and prices rose. JTPB with other land-owners felt the financial strain. Now the old manor-house was gone but the new castle because of the various construction problems was still barely habitable.

As a typical gentleman of Regency times, for JTPB there had been other expenses and distractions to leak away cash. During the

PORTHLUNEY COVE ... Scene of contraband runs that supplied the castle cellars.

early 1800s an advertisement had appeared in the Cornish papers stating that 'Bucephelos', a Derby winner, would be standing at stud at Caerhays on specified dates. No doubt such ventures brought in funds but many stories have survived of gambling and horse-racing and, less likely, cock-fighting in the castle grounds – a plebeian sport – ventures that seem to have proved largely non-profitable in the long run.

Porthluney Cove, just beyond the castle grounds, was for a long time the scene of activities of a successful smuggler, a certain Richard Kingcup who over many years frequently ran cargoes of brandy, tobacco, salt and silks onto local beaches. It was said that the gates of the castle nearest Porthluney beach were left discreetly ajar on moonlit nights at prearranged times, and no doubt there were capacious cellars in the new castle to be kept replenished at more or less reasonable cost. Certainly in time a watchhouse was built just along the cliff by the Coastguard authorities – necessitated by the lenient attitude of the Trevanions and other local gentry to fair-trading activities.

By 1824 the still incomplete castle in its picturesque setting, with half a hillside removed to make an ideal view from it towards the sea, became a new focus for tourist visitors to Cornwall. One of them, Stockdale, recorded in his book with, perhaps, a certain irony, since building had after all, first commenced in 1808, that: *'Carhayes was another beautiful mansion of castellated form lately rebuilt at a very considerable expense . . . and when perfectly finished will be as handsome a residence as any in the country . . .'*

Financial pressures now increased on JTPB. The experimental substance, likened by some to papier-maché, that Nash had used for the construction of the castle roof, had proved no match for a succession of stormy Cornish winters. To try to pay for all the repairs required, the whole manor of Caerhays and other Trevanion lands had to be mortgaged for the sum of £15,000. Only one straw showed which way a new wind of potential profit was blowing in Cornwall, but JTPB, like others, unfortunately ignored it. In 1827 in a bid to raise more funds he leased out for 21 years some land at Lower Ninestones on the ancient Treverbyn-Trevanion estate; lands held by Trevanions since Elizabethan times which had yielded over the years rich pickings in tin dues paid to the family. But the new lessees were the clay pioneers, Lovering, Martin and Nichols who contracted to pay to JTPB a quarter of the value of any clay raised. It was a fledgling industry at that time and thought little of by most but only 20 years later Treverbyn-Trevanion land proved to have the richest clay potential of all.

JTPB had family problems too to vex him. His second son Henry, born in 1804 and now in his 20s showed writing talent and at an early age had published a series of poems called *The Influence of Apathy*, that brought him acclaim as a young Cornish poet:

'Wild glimmering on the hearth, the blazing pile
Casts its warm light round the spacious hall
And many a ghost to superstitious eye
The distant shades in such abode would bring:
On either side the tarnished armour stands
On the thick walls with deep and varied tints,
Kings, mounted heroes and brocaded dames
In tapestry tell the deeds of other days,
While through the crevices the frequent gusts

Lift the torn clothes and wave their giant forms . . .'

Was this a description of the old manor house of the Trevanions or perhaps of the new castle in disrepair?

His second cousin, the poet Byron's influence is clear but Henry also wrote poems of a pious religiosity that were to seem ill-assorted with his later tempestuous life. For Henry married Georgiana, the daughter of Augusta Leigh, Byron's half sister, but only after he had had a brief affair with her susceptible mother. Three daughters were born to Georgiana in quick succession. Then, nothing subdued, Henry seduced his under-age sister-in-law, Medora, who was commonly supposed to be Byron's daughter by an incestuous relationship with Augusta. Medora was only 15 and soon pregnant too, the seduction by Henry having made great progress while the two were closeted together, piously studying the Bible.

Soon the inevitable scandal broke and, nothing loath, the guilty couple eloped to Brittany where a child was born in a nunnery but did not survive. Georgiana, the wronged wife, was hardly condemnatory and went to stay with them for a while in France thus adding to the couple's notoriety. For a time they made a home together in a ramshackle manor-house near Morlaix and there were frequent applications home to Caerhays for cash that almost certainly went unanswered by the hard-pressed JTPB. In time, after many temperamental quarrels, Medora departed and Henry was left to a solitary existence in the old house, until he finally died there all alone. As far as is known he wrote no more but ironically, one of his legitimate daughters was to inherit his talent and become a published poet herself in later, more respectable Victorian times.

So no help at all came to JTPB from his children and by 1839 things were in a bad way at the castle. A young Quaker businessman from Falmouth, Barclay Fox of the famous family there, recorded in his diary a family outing – a day trip in a trawler from Falmouth quay along the coast to land on Porthluney beach. He noted virtuously:

'. . . *Dined on board & landed at 1. Caerhays is a remarkable old place just this side the Deadman (*Dodman Point*). A fine rambling Gothic castle with turrets & towers in abundance, curiously situated near the sea, the late seat of Squire Trevanion whose style of living was that of a nobleman; he is now an outlaw & all his goods & chattels, House, Stock and Estate*

are brought to the hammer by Sheriff's order a melancholy moral on extrav-
agance & dissipation. The Sale was proceeding in the Stable yard. The only
things worthy of admiration were the house itself, the horse 'Marvel', the St
Bernard's dog a splendid & gentle creature & some of the bedsteads, the fur-
niture generally inferior & the library definitely 2nd rate . . .'

JTPB was probably no reader and the library, in a beautiful round room in one of the towers and specially designed by Nash was sadly run down. Perhaps all the best volumes had previously been extracted and sold.

But by this time JTPB had ignominiously fled the country to evade the bailiff's men. Mysteriously he then took up residence in Brussels alone and in the next year, 1840, he died leaving only £100 and very few possessions, all promptly seized by creditors there.

Back home at Caerhays the actual sale of the castle had not gone through because of legal problems over title deeds. John Charles Trevanion, JTPB's eldest son inherited but could do little to reme-dy matters. He lived in demoralised disorder in the castle which, by then, was hardly habitable at all. It was said that with his compan-ions his chief entertainment was shooting the eyes out of the family portraits that still hung on the draughty walls. Oddly one of these battered portraits actually survived to undergo repair at the present day.

Things went from bad to worse. The holes in the roof allowed puddles to appear on the drawing room floor on which ducks swam happily. In 1830 in a bid to augment his diminishing income JTPB had married a second wife who came from the more wealthy Burdett family. Now his son, John Charles, in a last desperate bid to save his inheritance invited his rich aunt Lady Burdett-Coutts to come down to Caerhays to stay. Her arrival in beneficent mood was soon fatally jarred when her uniformed footman announcing her arrival in the hall was viciously bitten by the castle dog (surely not the gentle St Bernard?). Through nervous reaction or possibly because of having imbibed too much in anticipation of his aunt's visit John Charles dissolved into helpless and hysterical laughter. He failed to produce the expected abject apology. Lady Burdett-Coutts called for her carriage and departed in an affronted fury – all hope of possible financial assistance from her for the beleaguered Trevanions now finally gone.

John Charles' sense of humour had not deserted him, it seems, even in this predicament as he had the portrait of the dog culprit carefully painted. The painting has survived and hangs in the castle today. There are also local tales of a fierce dog ghost in the grounds near the Battery overlooking the beach.

But now the only possible course of action was flight. It is said that as an army of bailiffs forced their way in through the tall gates between the two crenellated lodges guarding the entry to the bottom drive, the Trevanion family was forced to flee from the castle over the little river to the shelter of what is now known as Forty Acre Wood. From there, undetected, they left the castle and their estates for ever to make their escape by coach or sea away from the pursuing creditors. Brunel had not then bridged the Tamar so that the option of an escape made speedily by train upcountry from Cornwall was not then available to them.

In due course all was put up again for sale. In October 1852 at Dunns' Hotel in St. Austell the disposal of the Castle and all the Trevanion land-holdings that remained became a grand social

TURRETS AND TOWERS ... The castle presents an irregular but perfect silhouette.

event. Much moralising took place and there were rich rewards for all the more prudent local land-owners who sent their agents to bid and acquire what bargains they could.

The castle, forlorn but still beautiful in its state of disrepair, went for a song and its new owner, Michael Williams of Scorrier, found that it needed ten years of repairs before it was to be possible for his family to live there. All the ancient family lands later found so rich in clay made fortunes for new owners, but it was too late for the Trevanions of Caerhays who had to make new lives elsewhere. In the scattering of the family from their lands, and the resultant loss of identity historic family portraits and papers seem to have disappeared for ever. Though many junior branches of the family thrive to this day and are documented as living all over the world, the Caerhays Trevanions remained nostalgic for their lost Cornish heritage.

Then in the 1920s their last descendant, Hugh Eric Trevanion, seemingly effeminate and insecure, died in dubious circumstances after taking an overdose of his veronal sleeping draught. Dr Rowse describes how previously Hugh had made a tragi-comical visit to his former ancestral home, driving up uninvited to the castle front door, where his reception was cool due to the oddity of his manner and the unconventionality of his clothes. He had also made a will leaving all that remained of the family money, portraits and papers to his faithful 'companion'. After his death it seems that their fate is unknown.

But the castle at Caerhays remains, a gem of Regency architecture whose survival is due to the generations of the Williams family who also created the glorious gardens of rare plants that frame it today. Surely a true monument as well to one of the last of the Trevanions, JTPB, who had enough rash extravagant courage to try to create a reality out of a romantic dream.

WINDSWEPT TREES ... And the castle beyond.

REFERENCE
Denis Trevanion: The Trevanion Family History, 1987.
A.L. Rowse: The Byrons and the Trevanions, 1978.

About the author . .

DIANA MUDD – two words describe Diana Mudd – 'multi-talented'.

Born at Stoke Gabriel, South Devon, she went to school in Torquay before eventually making her way to Princetown where, in the heart of Dartmoor, she was to meet her husband David.

She has written – and had published – many poems. She paints – pictures as well as walls! – walks, skates, cycles; has modelled and taught dancing; designs gardens; is good at D-I-Y; and is an outstanding cook.

She has trained as a healer in the spiritual and psychic field, loves people and is a lover of the essence of life.

DIANA MUDD

SAVED TO SAVE OTHERS

Diana Mudd

A N OLD Cornishwoman and John Wesley used different words, and a different style of expression to note exactly the same thing about Cornish local preachers.

As Wesley put it, when visiting St. Agnes on Sunday September 4 1757: 'I could scarce have believed, if I had not heard it, that few men of learning write so correctly as an unlearned tinner speaks extempore'.

According to the Cornishwoman: 'Aw, ais, the loocals do very well. They're worken' all the day an' come night they're ready to drop; an' es 'ard for'm to maake up a sarmon. And then Sundays, see what miles they do walk for to get to all they by-plaaces, an' then lot o' them caan't read wan word in a book, but they're good men for all that. I don't knaw what we should do wethout the loocals'.

They had both noticed the strange fact that the more eloquent a local preacher might be, the less likely it was that he could read with ease or express his written thoughts clearly. Almost without exception, their inspiration and preaching skill was drawn from their experience of life; a few key texts learned during childhood and early manhood; and a simple but robust style of delivery. Many had survived fearful accidents; others were reformed drunkards; some had overcome physical temptation. They were united in the belief that they had been saved in order to save others from eternal damnation.

Without realising it, they used a very rough and ready psychology to get through to individual members of their congregations. Having sat and giggled (or nodded-off) in the pews themselves, they knew how to make a good point that would restore attention to the sermon.

One of the great Cornish hat-makers of the early 1800s was a Mr Cock. He proudly put a patch on the inside of the Sunday-best tall hats he made reminding anyone minded to look that they were the creation of 'Cock, Hatter'.

Knowing of the vanity of young men and their wish to possess one of Mr Cock's hats, one preacher took in the scene as he looked down from the pulpit. 'I know you, young men', he said. 'You kneel down and bow your heads to God, but all you see before your eyes is "Cock, Hatter". And you, young women, you are little better. Yes, when you pray you put up your hands to your eyes. But all the time you're taking a geek (having a peep) through your fingers in the hope your beau is come'.

It was into this world of spiritual eloquence without earthly education that Michael Verran was born, in mid-Cornwall, in 1808. He spent his late childhood in the tin mines of West Cornwall but, in 1838, moved to East Cornwall to work in the rich copper mines of the Tamar Valley, near St. Cleer.

In exchange for the salary of fifty shillings (£2.50) per month, Michael Verran worked six days a week. In addition to a ten or twelve-hour day, he had a round trip – on foot – of twenty miles daily merely to get to work and back.

One morning in August 1842, Michael went to work as usual at the South Caradon mine where, together with Peter Roberts and William Vial, he was helping to enlarge the main shaft which was already sixty feet deep.

They divided their jobs so that Vial stayed on the surface and raised or lowered the huge bucket that carried Roberts and Verran – one at a time – down or up the shaft. The bucket was also used to carry tools, explosives and rubble.

It was Verran's job to look after the tools and to clear the rubble after Roberts had set off necessary explosions. The routine was simple. As Roberts set the explosive and prepared the fuse, Verran collected the tools, joined them in the bucket, and went to the surface. Vial would then send the bucket down again. At this point, Roberts would light the fuse, get into the bucket and be winched to safety before the fuse ignited the explosive.

It was a fool-proof system . . . or so it seemed until that August morning. Verran sent the tools to the surface as Roberts lit a very long fuse. As it was so long, Verran waited longer than he should, not realising that Roberts was already shortening it to its usual length. As the cutting tools had already gone up the shaft, Roberts ignored all the safety rules by using a stone to pulverise the fuse so that he could twist it into a shorter length.

The stone he picked up in the semi-darkness was a flint! As it hit the fuse a spark was created and the smoking trail raced towards the gunpowder.

Without hesitation, Verran pushed Roberts into the bucket with the words: 'Go on, brother, I shall be in heaven in a minute'.

Vial hauled Roberts to the surface but before the bucket could be freed and sent back there was a colossal explosion of such severity that Roberts was slightly injured by flying stones thrown to the surface.

Through the settling dust they went down the shaft and looked at what they feared would be Verran's shattered body. It moved. Unbelievably they heard him say: 'Do not be afraid, I am not hurted'.

Verran's fame as a survivor and of having shown 'a noble instance of what a real Christian will do in the moment of extremity' spread and came to the attention of the great religious man of letters, Thomas Carlyle, who decided to try to help him. He asked his friend, John Sterling, to meet the miner and to find out 'What is there to be done for our benevolent friend . . . I am greatly against all "lion" prizes for virtue. At the same time one feels as if such a man as this miner were fit for something better than breaking stones at the bottom of a damp pit. I know not what can be done with him. If any subscription, or the like, were thought good, I would gladly give my poor guineas (£1.5p) among others. At all events, and if nothing further be done, I shall always know where a right brave man is living and labouring in this world along with me; and that itself is worth something'.

Sterling made contact with Verran and reported back that the miner had taken his place as a lay-preacher and that he was trying to save £40 or £50 so that he could take six months off work to try to learn to read and write to help his ministry.

Carlyle was delighted. He contacted all the leading Cornish families and they jointly sent £25 to 'a right brave man, and highly wor-

INDUSTRIAL HERITAGE ... Ponies graze in the former mining country around St Cleer.

thy to be educated, these small gifts of money, if they can assist him therein, are, with all hopefulness and good regard, presented by certain fellow wayfarers and warfarers of his'.

Caroline Fox, of Falmouth, took a close interest in Verran's conversion to active Methodism and she told Carlyle that he 'sometimes feels so full of joy that his skin feels too small for him, and he is obliged to lie down and pray that he may be enlarged to make room for his bursting happiness'.

He spent his £25 wisely by buying a small dairy business. This gave him the time and the income to study reading and writing and even basic theology from other churchmen.

But, despite his increase in worldly knowledge, his sermons still kept the basic simplicity of a man who, through being saved from death, had found his own soul and his true purpose in life.

Shortly after his death, this simple explanation of having found himself was discovered among his various notes and jottings, in June 1862:

'When I think of God's goodness to me I am ready to cry out O wat a detter for both temporal and spiritual blessings. My path is like that of just shining briter and briter but I must confess I am a brand pluckd from the eternal burning but thanks be to the Lord I am more than concueror through him that so loved me and the language of my heart is O that my head was water and mine eyes a fountain of tears that I might weep day and night . . .I am determining at this time to be spend and to be spent on the Glory of God may he ever keep me humble'.

As Thomas Carlyle said of the unskilled, untrained, uneducated miner and preacher: 'It seemed to me that I had not lately fallen in with a man's fuller piece of heroism, of swift conclusive insight into what was fit to be done, and resolution to do it, than in the case of the poor self-immolating miner'.

If Michael Verran's conversion was based on one incident, that of Billy Bray was at the end of a long and unhappy route when, as 'formerly a drunken and lascivious miner, I was transformed by the Truth and Spirit of God into a loving and consistent disciple of the Son of God'.

Born at Twelveheads, between Truro and Falmouth, on June 1 1794, he spent more of his early life in the village inn than in the chapel. He later admitted that his life was 'very bad, the nearest thing to Hell. I drank all night long and had a sore head, a sick stomach and, worse than all, such horrors of mind that no tongue can tell'.

His escape from these horrors was dramatic and immediate. He came home from work, one evening in November 1823, sober for

BALDHU CHURCH
WHERE BILLY BRAY IS BURIED

BILLY BRAY

"THE KING'S SON".

A NOTABLE
CORNISH MINER
AND PREACHER.

Born & Died
at
Twelve Heads.
IN THE PARISH OF KEA
NEAR TRURO.

AGED 73 YEARS

IN MEMORY OF
WILLIAM BETTER KNOWN AS
BILLY BRAY.
WHO DIED AT TWELVE HEADS.
MAY 25TH 1868,
AGED SEVENTY-THREE YEARS.

MONUMENT ERECTED AT BALDHU
OVER THE GRAVE OF BILLY BRAY

75

the first time. His pay was intact. He gave his wife all the money he had earned for the week and told her: 'By the help of the Lord you will never see me drunk nor smoking again'.

He kept his promise about drinking, but weakened in his smoking. Like many of the poorer people of Cornwall he suffered from bad teeth and often returned to his pipe in the belief that the smoke would help soothe the inevitable and painful bouts of toothache that were a regular fact of life.

He started attending the chapel at Twelveheads and eventually became a much-loved and highly-respected local preacher. For some unexplained reason he associated himself with St. Peter. He described chapels as being nets for souls.

One day it occurred to him that he would like to build his own chapel. His mother gave him the land, just across the road from his home where, as he said: 'In the neighbourhood where I lived, there were a great many, dark-minded, wicked people and chapels were few. The Lord put it into my mind to build one'.

It was a massive task. He worked long hours in the mine and, tired and exhausted at the end of the shift, he begged and borrowed materials, hauled stone and worked late into the night to build his chapel. Some other preachers turned against him in his committed work. People laughed at him. 'Most of them turned against me and tried to set the preachers against me', he said later, 'but all they could do, they could not hurt me, though they made me uneasy at times'.

Local wags suggested that he should fit a chimney so that, if he could not find a congregation, he could at least own a cottage. He answered that he would have no chimney 'other than to drive the devil through'.

He persevered and he succeeded. He named his chapel 'Bethel' and said: 'Many will have to bless God forever that Bethel chapel was built, for many are in heaven that were born there'.

He prophesied: 'If this new chapel stands one hundred years, and one soul be converted in it every year, that will be one hundred souls; and one soul is worth more than all Cornwall'.

He built more chapels. He continued to work as a miner. He travelled as a preacher. He never stopped.

He was a short, swarthy man with bright eyes, sharp features and a strong mouth. He usually preached in white miner's trousers, miner's boots, a long black coat, and with his red miner's handkerchief around his throat. He would carry his miner's hat with its broad leather crown and would tell his congregation to come with him to heaven. 'If there is one crown short, take mine for I will willingly go without one'.

He would use his handkerchief to make an impact. He would wrap it gently around the Bible and then throw it to the floor, warning that the descent to Hell would be as rapid and inevitable if true repentance was not sought or offered.

His meetings were as dramatic as the rallies, a century and a half later, of Billy Graham. At one which lasted for the best part of eight days, there was an attendance of an estimated three thousand people.

BIRTHPLACE VILLAGE ... Cottages at Twelveheads, Billy Bray was born in the small village in 1794 and died there 73 years later.

*IN HIS MEMORY ... The Methodist chapel at Carharrack built in 1883
to commemorate Billy Bray.*

'After I had announced my text, a mighty power of the spirit of
God came upon the people, and many began to cry aloud for mercy.
It was soon impossible to go on preaching, so I gave out a hymn and

went amongst "the slain of the Lord". The men and women in distress were led into the schoolroom. As one and another found peace we asked them to go out and let others come in. In this way I went on until ten o'clock. It will scarcely be credited, but that meeting was prolonged without intermission day or night for eight days after it began'.

Certainly he possessed outstanding physical fitness and amazing strength. He would trudge twenty miles on a Sunday to keep two preaching appointments. Then, in the fervour of his preaching, he would leave the pulpit, descend on an unsuspecting worshipper and carry him or her around the chapel in a frenzied dance, asking 'Is not this pretty riding, my dear?'.

Once he met a tramp. Although not a wealthy man himself, he exchanged his own clothes with the tattered garments the vagrant had been given somewhere else. When he arrived home his wife told him off for his folly.

'The Lord will provide', he said, diving his hand into his pocket and producing a coin that had slipped into the lining before the coat had been given to the tramp.

One of the reasons he was so loved was because he was so down to earth. One morning he was late for a service. The organist filled in with the only three or four hymns he could play, but Billy did not turn up. The organist and the congregation started a musical lap of honour.

The door opened, Billy Bray dashed in and made for the pulpit. He told the amazed congregation: 'Sorry I am late, my friends. I got held up on the way'. Then, by way of further explanation: 'Loose bowels, you know'.

One of his chapels needed a pulpit. But there was no money for it. He went to a sale and spotted a huge wardrobe. He saw who bought it and followed the purchaser home. There he persuaded him that it was totally unsuited to the room for which it was intended and was not only given it, but he also persuaded the buyer to give him 7s. 6d. (37½p) to have it delivered to the chapel and cut down into a pulpit.

His love of life often caused him to break into impromptu dances. When he was told that it wasn't the done thing for a preacher to dance, he reminded his critics that, according to the Bible, David was another dancer. 'David, you know, was a king. Well, bless the Lord, I'm the King's son'.

Criticising himself and other pipe smokers for their weakness, he said that it was not part of God's plan that man should smoke: 'If our good Father meant for men to smoke', he said, 'He'd 've put a hole in the top of their heads; for 'tisn't no heavenly architect as'd leave the smoke go out the front door'.

Towards the end of his life he found walking a growing discomfort and, as a compromise between visiting congregations or expecting them to visit him, he had a solid wooden chair built so that he could be carried if he grew tired. It was, as he said, his equivalent of a bishop's crook.

He lived until he was 74, eventually passing to his expected paradise on May 25 1868. He lies buried at Baldhu, looking down on his beloved Carnon valley under a splendid memorial recalling his 'sanctified wit' and his example to his fellow men.

It was an example that those without qualifications may often be the best teachers; that love can create learning; and that wit can be as effective as wisdom.

Once, calling on one of his congregation who had missed a few services and seemed to be avoiding him, be obviously arrived at a bad time.

After sounds of considerable scuffling inside the cottage, the door was opened by a little girl who seemed ill-at-ease. She smiled and bobbed her knee to him. 'Mother says as 'ow she'd 've liked for to see 'e Mr Bray, but 'er's just 'ad for to go out'. 'That's all right', he said, glancing towards the bottom of the half-opened door. 'But you'd better tell her that next time she do go out, she ought for to take 'er feet with 'er'.

STONE MEMORIAL ... Billy Bray is buried in the churchyard at Baldhu.

About the author ...

MICHAEL WILLIAMS, a Cornishman, started full-time publishing in 1975. He and his wife Sonia live in a cottage on the shoulder of a green valley just outside St. Teath in North Cornwall.

In addition to publishing and writing, Michael Williams is a keen cricketer and collector of cricket books and autographs. He was the first captain of the Cornish Crusaders Cricket Club and is today President of the Crusaders. He is also a member of Cornwall and Gloucestershire County Cricket Clubs. A member of the RSPCA and the International League for the Protection of Horses, he has worked hard for reform in laws relating to animal welfare. In 1984 he was elected to The Ghost Club, and is convinced Cornwall is the most haunted area in the whole of Great Britain.

His Bossiney titles include Supernatural Search in Cornwall, Superstition & Folklore, *and* Paranormal in the Westcountry. *As a publisher he now operates in six areas: Cornwall, Devon, Somerset, Avon, Dorset and Wiltshire. He is currently working on* Curious Cornwall.

HAUNTED CORNWALL

Michael Williams

GHOSTS are as old as recorded history, and here in Cornwall they are numerous and various.

It is my considered opinion the evidence for ghosts is so strong that the only area for doubt and debate centres on the *nature* of ghosts. Spiritualists, of course, maintain ghosts are the spirits of people who have departed this earthly life. Alan Nance, the well-known Spiritualist and healer of St. Austell, told me how he had talked, at great length, with a knight from an earlier century who was still roaming Cornwall looking for his lost horse all those years ago.

In this chapter I am concentrating on Supernatural happenings in Cornwall – all appearing in book form for the first time.

The first account comes from David Mudd, MP for Falmouth and Camborne for 22 years. Writing to me in December 1991, he recalled: 'I had driven the six-hour journey from London to Falmouth in a mixture of darkness and driving sleet and snow flurries. I was very tired and when the following happened, I put it down to tiredness.'

'Driving along Woodlane to the top of Swanpool Street, I became aware of a man coming towards me seemingly pushing a cart. He was wearing a long coat of the 17th century. I thought it a little weird, but it was such a cold night that anyone could be excused for wearing anything! As I drew level with him, he pulled into the side of the road as if to let me pass. Once past him, I instinctively looked in the mirror and saw him cross the road behind me and go through the wall into the coach-yard of Grove Hill House.

'There's one rather important point, though . . . the wall is unbroken at that point and there is no gate or doorway.

'A couple of years ago I was talking to an old friend from Falmouth, Captain John Masson. Completely out of the blue, he asked me if I knew of any ghosts in Falmouth. I asked him why.

' "Well", he said, "I think I may have seen one. Passing through Woodlane, I saw a man in an old-fashioned coat pushing what looked like a cart. He crossed the road and disappeared into the wall of Grove Hill House".'

Story number two also concerns Falmouth, only a few hundred yards from Woodlane, and here I am indebted to *Western Morning News* journalist Louise Midgley.

In November 1991, old bones, suspected of belonging to a child, were discovered under the floor of a haunted building in the town. They were found in a 1920s style building at Hulls Lane which now belongs to Trago Mills.

The blackened bones were discovered when workmen renovating the building pulled up some rotten floorboards. Two detectives were called from Penryn and the bones were taken to Treliske Hospital, Truro, for identification. There they were identified as those of a seal. What the bones of a seal were doing under the floorboards of a built-up area of Falmouth must remain a Cornish mystery.

Curiosity stirred, I contacted Tony Acton-Page, the Trago manager at Falmouth who assured me 'a shadowy figure, believed to be that of a man, had been seen on several occasions by several different people over the years . . . moving across a landing at the top of the building.'

Then in January 1992 I received this letter from the United States:

'Dear Michael, I have just finished reading your book *Cornish Mysteries*. Since you seem to get information from friends for your writings, I decided to appoint myself a friend and relate what happened to me in Cornwall in 1990.

'To introduce myself; I am Robert Metcalf, an American whose ancestors came from Wensleydale in Yorkshire, so I am in no way Cornish. I did however have the good fortune to marry a girl whose family comes from Scorrier, Cornwall.

'I have a BS in Physical Science so I am a rather solid non-believing person when it comes to ghosts. I do have precognition, but seldom and it is never completely right.

'My wife and I were spending a week staying with my wife's cousin in the old family farm house in Whealrose. We stayed in an upstairs bedroom which made for a long trip to the loo. I did not feel alone as I made my nightly trips. Whatever was there did not like my being there.

'Halfway through the second trip I encountered a figure walking briskly past a doorway I was approaching and through my torch beam. Since the house was securely locked, no one could be there. I jumped quickly forward with my torch and found the dead end hallway empty.

'The next morning I asked my artist wife to draw a picture from my description. She and I both did this and produced quite similar drawings. Here are her notes written the next morning: "Bob's ghost – Landsdowne, Cornwall – small, dark grey, solid, no features except a peak on the head like a cap, and a nose – moved quickly from the Cornish kitchen into the front hall to disappear."

'This figure was walking from left to right across the open doorway. It was solid and could not be seen through. There was no sound accompanying it. The next day when I measured its height against pictures on the wall it seemed to have been about four and a half feet tall.

'Later in the week I saw figures for sale to the tourists that had the same head outline. This was caused by a cap. The rest of the figures did not fit at all being short and fat. I was told they were called piskies and represented Cornish "little people."

'After this episode I no longer felt a negative presence in the house. Instead I had a feeling of welcome from the old house. The lady cousin said that it was a happy house and there had never been a mention of ghosts. She feels comfortable living there.'

Our next episode comes from Meg Fossey of Illogan, Redruth.

'I went back to the house the other day. It was the first time for 36 years. I had been on a visit to Kehelland and driving back to Camborne I happened to notice the side turning that led to it. I pulled up and reversed back. I hesitated for a moment, "Should I or shouldn't I?" A few minutes later I found myself parked opposite the front gate.

'I gazed at the front of the house and wondered what all the fuss had been about all those years ago. It looked perfectly innocuous, like everyone's dream of the perfect cottage in the country. It was set alone in a secluded spot in a quiet country lane. A typical double-fronted Cornish granite cottage with a sheltered garden fronted by two huge privet hedges.

'I got out of the car and walked over to the front gate. My eyes were irresistibly drawn to the middle bedroom window. I noted with surprise that there was a baby's cot placed under it in exactly the same position as my bed used to be. Perhaps babies are not susceptible to ghosts? Or maybe it has left? However, I could hardly

MEG FOSSEY

walk up to the front door and say, "Excuse me but I used to live here as a girl and I've just called back to ask if you still have a ghost in the box room". After a few moments I walked back to my car and drove home.

'My father had been in business in London but was in bad health and had been advised by the doctor to move to the country. We arrived at the house in January 1955. We three children tumbled out of the car beside ourselves with excitement. I ran into the middle bedroom, a small box room, and announced to my younger siblings that I had bagged the room for myself. I arranged my few possessions on the wide windowsill and sat looking out over the fields opposite feeling as though I was in paradise.

'But I didn't settle as well as the rest of the family. I felt depressed and unhappy. My parents put it down to the sudden change of environment. After all, I was 17 and we had moved from a large town and I had left all my friends behind. But it seemed to be more than that. Just before bedtime I would begin to feel a strange sense of unease and when I started to climb the stairs to bed I found it physically difficult to put one foot in front of the other. It was as if some strange force over which I had no control, was trying to prevent me from climbing the stairs.

'Very soon after this I was awakened one night by the sound of heavy breathing close to my ear. I went to sit up but felt as though I was bound hand and foot with fine cord. I could do nothing but endure it until I fell asleep. The next morning I put the whole experience down to a nightmare. However, the nightmare continued and night after night I would wake to feel a malevolent "presence" beside my bed breathing in my ear. I began to feel more and more terrified and spent as little time as I could in my room.

'I wanted to confide in my parents but I felt that they would put it down to my teenage imagination. At last my terror overcame my reservations and I told my mother. To my immense surprise she quickly moved me out of the room and put my seven-year-old brother in there. Within the year we had moved from our "dream cottage" into a town house in Camborne. As is the way with youth, I soon forgot about the whole incident.

'Some years later, in the 70s, I was standing at the bar in The Trevithick Arms in Camborne having a drink with my younger brother. He waved at someone across the room and said: "That's so and so, he lives in our old house at Treswithian". I looked back at the man curiously and said: "I wonder what they do about . . .", and before I had a chance to finish my sentence my brother cut in with – "The room". I looked at him in astonishment. "So you know?"

' "Well, I should think so, after all I had to sleep in it after you, I was bloody terrified."

' "What happened to you?"

' "I used to hear this awful breathing near my ear and have a feeling of being bound and helpless. Then there was this big black dog sitting on the end of the bed looking at me. I felt it was going to pounce on me at any moment."

' "A dog? I never saw a dog, just the awful breathing and the trapped sensation. So it wasn't my imagination then?"

'Several drinks later we plucked up the courage to go over to the man who now lived in the house. We brought the conversation around to the fact that we had lived there for a short while and then carefully broached the subject of the room. He laughed and said: "I know what you are referring to, we have a simple way of dealing with it, we just don't go in it".

'Several more years passed and I was visiting my father who lives at Condurrow. He is in his 80s and loves to reminisce. We got around to the house at Treswithian and I started to tell him of my experience when he interrupted me. "Yes I know", he said. "It's the reason we moved from there so fast. Your mother came to me and told me how you felt. I didn't believe it of course, so after we moved you out, and your brother in, I went into the room some nights later after he had fallen asleep, and sat on the bed. After about ten minutes I got up to leave when I was overcome with a choking sensation and a feeling of great heaviness in my chest. There was also a deep feeling of a black indescribable fear, yet an inability to move. It took all my willpower to walk out of that door and down the stairs. I went into the living room and said to your mother, "We're putting the house on the market tomorrow".'

I am sometimes asked 'which, in your opinion, is the most haunted place in Cornwall?'

I have no hesitation in replying: 'St. Nectan's Glen.'

St. Nectan's Glen is on the landward side of the Tintagel-Boscastle road. At the head of the glen is the Hermitage, said to be the site of the Saint's cell which today is the Hermitage Tea Gardens. Nearby a waterfall thunders through a natural arch, plunges over a stone obstacle, falls more than forty feet and races away down the glen.

It was in the spring of 1965 that I first came here. Since then I have compiled a substantial file on strange happenings hereabouts.

Monk-like figures, suddenly appearing and suddenly disappearing; chanting at night; the ghost of a living person seen not once, but twice; music from an invisible musician; the vanishing of a Supernatural building – 'there one night and gone the next morning' – weird, mocking laughter, cats fighting invisible enemies. Only when the owner of the property recently gave me this short account did a realization strike home.

In 1991 Barry Litton and his wife decided to go away for a few days and asked a friend to come and stay at the Hermitage to keep an eye on the place and feed the animals.

'At one point he went outside to feed the rabbits and there standing on the plateau overlooking the waterfall was the figure of a monk – so real, so life-like – that our caretaker friend said "I don't wish you any harm." There was no reply but there was no doubt in his mind that he had really seen a monk.'

That latest sighting is 27 years after the first account I recorded. In those 27 years I have interviewed 13 people – six women and seven men – who have had experiences in the glen, all defying logical explanation. And perhaps most interesting of all, my recorded sightings of monks in grey by people interviewed covers a period of more than forty years. This is an extraordinary sequence and I frankly find it hard to believe all those individuals were deluded.

The great majority of people go through life without a single Supernatural experience. Others have just one experience, and a small number keep having Supernatural sightings – one such character is David Waddon-Martyn who lives at The Old Millfloor, Trebarwith near Tintagel. I first interviewed David back in the 1960s.

This following account, however, covers entirely new ground – and is especially interesting in that sightings of groups of people are relatively rare. Here is David Waddon-Martyn's detailed recollection:

'This most definitely was a sighting on the cliffs of Morwenstow between Sharpnose Point and the Tonecombe Downs near to Stanbury beach. The time of year was very late summer. It was a nice sunny afternoon . . . and I was out shooting rabbits. I was amongst gorse and heather not far off the coastal footpath.

'I was suddenly aware of a group of youngsters (four young

MONK-LIKE FIGURE … The strange apparition seen at St Nectan's Glen.

women and four young men) advancing up the footpath from the direction of Sharpnose Point.

'I watched six of them climb a stile (three women and three men) and walk several yards along the path by the cliff edge and then they all sat down. One young couple had broken away and ventured further into the gorse and heather area, but then they went out of sight from where I was sitting.

'After possibly five minutes, the six people sitting on the cliff top made a move as if to walk down the cliff where there is a small stream running down the cliff face (very, very steep). They disappeared – no screams, nothing, and on my way to where I last saw them there was no sign of anyone and no sign of the other couple. I am totally convinced this was a sighting. I would have definitely seen all the parties concerned had they been of this place and time, and I am sure any human (alive and well) would never have gone down the cliff in this particular spot which is a sheer 400 ft.

'It was very strange. I was at the beginning under the impression they were all out for a walk and were simply normal until this occurred. The date was 1980.'

Many 'sightings' occur when the individual's mind is far from the Supernatural. David Waddon-Martyn was out for an afternoon's shooting, and this next account from Mr G.H. Walke of Exeter shows how he and his friends had their mind on King Arthur:

'On Friday 23 August, 1991 I travelled from Exeter to Boscastle and Tintagel, with three friends, on a little sightseeing and exploration trip. Later, when we left to make our way homewards to Exeter, we decided to stop at Slaughter Bridge, and find the stone which was reputed to be Arthur's grave.

'We drove up a private lane, and parked the car opposite a path which sloped downwards to the stream. Only a small stream was flowing, so we were able to step down about two feet on to the river bed gravel and walk toward Arthur's stone.

'After carefully examining the large block of stone and trying to read the inscribed Latin, we made our way back the way we came.

'A little way along the path a tree blocked the way, and my friends followed the path around it. As I approached the tree with my head down, looking out for obstacles, I glanced upwards and saw a couple, a man with his back to the tree embracing a woman who wore a dark crimson dress or gown which reached to her ankles. I had the impression that the man was dressed in dark grey.

'They did not seem to notice me, and not wanting to seem rude and curious, I bent my head down again and passed around the tree, not even bothering to look backwards. One often sees couples embracing in public these days and I did not give the incident another thought, and continued on my way.

'I was the last to reach the roadway and nearing the top of the path encountered a party of about half a dozen people making their way downwards. They had a transit type van with a German registration, so I assumed they were Germans and that the couple I had seen further down was part of their party, enjoying a quick kiss and a cuddle.

'We drove back to Exeter and I did not think of the embracing couple until my friends were making their farewells. It was then I mentioned seeing them. To my astonishment and disbelief they told me that there had not been anyone there on the path! We discussed the matter and I had to admit that the lady's dress was quite inappropriate for a walk down the path towards the stream, it would have been badly torn. The conclusion we came to was that I had seen an apparition of some sort.

'The time was 4.30 p.m. the couple appeared quite solid, and I came close enough to have touched them if I had so wished. I regret now that I did not stare and try to see their faces. The only impression I have is that they were tall and slim.'

Our final account comes from across the Atlantic and there is a Cornish connection in that the story was passed to me by Marilyn Preston Evans, the well-known healer and UFO researcher of Saltash.

Joyce Tolliver of Bedford (USA) was driving her five children to a park when one of her car tyres 'blew.' It was a rural section of road with little passing traffic; so she was relieved to see a motorcyclist pull up as she tried to change the tyre.

'The smiling young man had the bluest eyes I have ever seen,' she recalled. 'Immediately, he offered to help. The boy worked very quickly, but I noticed one strange thing. Even though it was very hot, he never broke into a sweat. When he finished changing the tyre, I asked him his name.' Joyce offered the young man some money, but he declined saying 'There's no need for that. In fact where I'm going I don't need money.' He got back on to his motor cycle and drove off down the empty road, disappearing as quickly as he had come.

That evening Joyce told her husband about the young man and they agreed he deserved the money that he had turned down. They called 'information' and asked for the listings of the last name Joyce had written down. After a few calls, a woman answered the phone.

When Joyce asked if she had a son by the first name written down, the woman replied: 'Yes.' Then, as Joyce began to tell the story of the tyre change, the woman began to cry. 'She asked me to describe him. I told her he had sandy hair, and mentioned a high school class ring he was wearing – and especially described his deep blue eyes.'

Composing herself the woman at the end of the telephone explained: 'My son was killed on that road just over a year ago. The motor cycle you describe is the gift my husband and I bought him for graduation!'

This is truly a remarkable account on two scores. First, a rare example of interaction between a living person and a ghost, and secondly, the spirit person doing something positively constructive for people in the here and now.

MORE BOSSINEY BOOKS . . .

MYSTERIES IN THE CORNISH LANDSCAPE
by **Tamsin Thomas** of Radio Cornwall

A tour of thirty historic locations in Cornwall by the well-known Cornish broadcaster, starting at Chun Castle down in the Hundred of Penwith and ending at The Hurlers on the eastern edge of Bodmin Moor.

'Tamsin takes us on an enjoyable and speculative canter – literally for she is often on horseback – through these fascinating and often controversial features of old Kernow.'

Donald Rawe, **Cornish Scene**

'Tamsin has produced a delightful book which will enchant her audience.'

Ronnie Hoyle, **The Western Morning News**

AROUND & ABOUT THE SMUGGLERS' WAYS
by **David Mudd**

Working through almost forty different sources, including the records of H.M. Customs & Excise itself, David Mudd (who discovered in the course of his research that his great-grandfather was a Customs officer) has produced a book that is as heady and addictive as the spirits, the wines and the tobaccos that once followed fish, tin and copper as Cornwall's great industries. Several of the sketches and many of the photographs are by David's wife, Diana.

'. . . scrapes the romantic glitter from Cornwall's erstwhile illicit trade . . . Meticulously researched and written in David Mudd's lively factual style it makes absorbing reading.'

Alison Poole, **Leader Group of Newspapers**

DAPHNE DU MAURIER COUNTRY
by **Martyn Shallcross**

A special look at Cornwall in which the internationally-famous novelist set important stories.

'A treasure chest for those who love Cornwall and the du Maurier novels.'

Valerie Mitchell, **The Packet Group of Newspapers**

SUPERSTITION AND FOLKLORE
by **Michael Williams**

A survey of Westcountry Superstitions: interviews on the subject and some Cornish and Devon folklore.

'. . . the strictures that we all ignore at our peril. To help us to keep out of trouble, Mr Williams has prepared a comprehensive list.' Frank Kempe, **North Devon Journal-Herald**

We shall be pleased to send you our catalogue giving full details of our growing list of titles for Devon, Cornwall, Dorset, Somerset and Wiltshire and forthcoming publications. If you have difficulty in obtaining our titles, write direct to Bossiney Books, Land's End, St. Teath, Bodmin, Cornwall.